Rookie
Read-About®
Science

Sound

Cody Crane

Content Consultant
Elizabeth Case DeSantis, M.A. Elementary Education
Julia A. Stark Elementary School, Stamford, Connecticut

Reading Consultant
Jeanne M. Clidas, Ph.D.
Reading Specialist

Children's Press®
An Imprint of Scholastic Inc.

Library of Congress Cataloging-in-Publication Data
Names: Crane, Cody, author.
Title: Sound/by Cody Crane.
Other titles: Rookie read-about science.
Description: New York, NY: Children's Press, an imprint of Scholastic
Inc., [2019] | Series: Rookie read-about science
Identifiers: LCCN 2018027641| ISBN 9780531134115 (library
binding) | ISBN 9780531138052 (pbk.)
Subjects: LCSH: Sound—Juvenile literature.
Classification: LCC QC225.5 .C765 2019 | DDC 534—dc23

Produced by Spooky Cheetah Press
Design: Brenda Jackson
Digital Imaging: Bianca Alexis
Creative Direction: Judith E. Christ for Scholastic Inc.
© 2019 by Scholastic Inc. All rights reserved.

Published in 2019 by Children's Press, an imprint of
Scholastic Inc.

Printed in Heshan, China   62

1 2 3 4 5 6 7 8 9 10 R 28 27 26 25 24 23 22 21 20 19

Scholastic Inc., 557 Broadway, New York,
NY 10012

Photographs ©:cover: Hendrata Yoga Surya/EyeEm/Getty
Images; back cover: Barbara Helgason/Dreamstime; 2-3:
Caia Images/Superstock; 5: Silke Woweries/Getty Images; 6:
Steve Hamblin/Alamy Images; 6 dog: James Levin Studios;
9: PhotoAlto/Matthieu Spohn/Getty Images; 10: Africa
Studio/Shutterstock; 13: JGI/Jamie Grill/Getty Images; 15:
Gordon Baer/Black Star/Newscom; 17: Klein and Hubert/
Minden Pictures; 18: Mark Taylor/Nature Picture Library; 19:
Barbara Helgason/Dreamstime; 21: RubberBall/Superstock;
22, : amophoto_au/Shutterstock; 25: Ingrid Visser/SeaPics.
com; 27 top left: Ian Boddy/Science Source; 27 top right:
monkeybusinessimages/iStockphoto; 27 bottom: Cultura
RM Exclusive/Sporrer/Rupp/Getty Images; 28, 29: www.
RaisingLifelongLearners.com; 30 top: Ian Boddy/Science
Source; 30 center: Barbara Helgason/Dreamstime; 30
bottom: Steve Hamblin/Alamy Images; 30 bottom dog: James
Levin Studios; 31 top: Gordon Baer/Black Star/Newscom;
31 center: Africa Studio/Shutterstock; 31 bottom: Klein and
Hubert/Minden Pictures; 32: imageBROKER/Superstock.

Table of Contents

Chapter 1

Listen Up

SHHHHHHHHHHHHHH!
Be as quiet as you can.
Now listen.
What do you hear?

5

Maybe you heard a car horn honking or a dog barking. Or maybe you heard music playing or people talking. All of these are types of **sounds**.

What are some reasons a dog might bark?

Sounds can be loud or soft.
They can last a long time
or come in short bursts.

What type of sound do you hear when a balloon pops?

9

Chapter 2

Good Vibrations

Things create sounds when they **vibrate**. That is when something moves back and forth. Strumming a guitar causes its strings to vibrate. The vibration creates a sound.

You can sometimes see these vibrations. You can sometimes feel them, too. Try touching something that is making a sound.

What might you feel if you touch a pot that has been hit?

13

A **tuning fork** shows how vibrations make sound. This metal tool has two arms. They vibrate when hit. That makes one clear note you can hear.

Why must you first hit a tuning fork to make a sound?

15

Making Waves

When something vibrates, it causes the air around it to move. When sound moves up and down in the air, it creates a sound **wave**. You cannot see it. But a sound moves through the air just like a ripple in a pond.

Sound waves travel through the air to your **ears**. The waves cause small bones inside your ear to vibrate. Animals' ears work the same way.

How might big ears help an animal hear better?

19

The vibrations send a message to your brain. Then your brain tells you what you hear.

Does music sound different when you listen to it through headphones?

Chapter 4

Getting Around

Sound can travel long distances. That is why you can hear noises that happen far away. It takes time for the sound of fireworks going off to reach your ears.

Would fireworks sound louder if they were closer to you?

Sound can move through things besides air. It can move through water. And it can move through a solid object like a wall or door.

Why might dolphins need to hear sounds underwater?

Sometimes we want sounds to travel even farther. So people have come up with **devices** to talk over long distances.

What
makes
sound an
important part
of your
daily life?

string telephone

telephone

megaphone

27

Make a String Telephone

Call a friend, using a phone you make!

Remember to ask an adult for help with this activity.

1. Poke a small hole in the bottom of each of two large paper or plastic cups. Cut a long length of string.

2. Thread one end of the string through the hole in each cup. Tie a knot in the ends of the string.

3. Put one cup over your ear. Have another person talk into the other cup. What do you hear?

What Happened?

When someone talks into one of your string phone's cups, his or her voice vibrates the air inside. The vibrations travel along the string to the other cup as sound you can hear!

devices (dih-**vise**-ez): tools created to help people do specific tasks

- *Some **devices** let people talk over long distances.*

ears (eerz): body parts used to hear sounds

- *Dogs have two **ears** that allow them to listen to sounds.*

sounds (soundz): things you can hear

- *Honking car horns make loud **sounds**.*

tuning fork (toon-ing fork): a metal tool with two arms that plays a note when struck

- *Striking a **tuning fork** creates one clear note.*

vibrate (vye-brate): to quickly move back and forth

- *Guitar strings **vibrate** when you strum them.*

wave (wayv): a swell that moves through air or water

- *Splashing creates a **wave** that ripples through the water.*

Facts for Now

Visit this Scholastic website for more information on Sound and to download the Reader's Guide for this series:
http://www.factsfornow. scholastic.com
Enter the keyword **Sound**

About the Author

Cody Crane is an award-winning children's science writer. She lives in Texas with her husband and son.